What's That Smell?

▪ A KIDS' GUIDE TO KEEPING CLEAN ▪

by Rachelle Kreisman

with illustrations by Tim Haggerty

RED
CHAIR
▪PRESS▪

Please visit our website at **www.redchairpress.com** for more high-quality products for young readers.

What's That Smell?

Publisher's Cataloging-In-Publication Data
(Prepared by The Donohue Group, Inc.)

Kreisman, Rachelle, author.
What's that smell? : a kids' guide to keeping clean / by Rachelle Kreisman ; with illustrations by Tim Haggerty.

pages : illustrations ; cm. -- (Start smart: health)

Includes bibliographical references and index.

Summary: Dogs do it. Birds do it. Even stinky skunks do it! Keeping your body clean is one of the most important ways we all get along. Learn why it's important to your health, and the health of others, to stay clean and cut down on the stink!
ISBN: 978-1-937529-67-3 (library hardcover)
ISBN: 978-1-937529-66-6 (paperback)
ISBN: 978-1-937529-88-8 (ebook)

1. Hygiene--Juvenile literature. 2. Cleanliness. I. Haggerty, Tim, illustrator. II. Title.

RA777 .K745 2014

613/.0432   2013956242

Illustration credits: p. 1, 3, 5, 7, 10, 11, 13, 15, 16, 17, 18, 20, 25, 27, 29, 30, 31: Tim Haggerty

Photo credits: Cover: Yellow Dog Productions/Getty Images; p. 4, 5, 6, 7, 15, 16, 17, 19, 20, 21, 22, 23, 24, 25, 26: IStock; p. 4, 5, 9, 10, 11, 12, 13, 14, 15, 18, 23: Shutterstock; p. 32: Courtesy of the author, Rachel Kreisman

This series first published by:
Red Chair Press LLC   PO Box 333   South Egremont, MA 01258-0333

Printed in the United States of America

1 2 3 4 5 18 17 16 15 14

Table of Contents

Words in **bold type** are defined in the glossary.

CHAPTER 1

Your Amazing Skin

S*niff. Sniff.* Do you smell that? It may be you! The human body works hard. It gets dirty, sweaty, oily, and stinky. No problem though—you can smell great and feel fresh in no time. All you need to do is practice good **hygiene**. That means keeping your body clean to stay healthy.

How does the body get so dirty? It all starts with the biggest **organ** of your body—your skin! Skin is amazing. It covers your body and protects your insides. Skin stretches and lets you move. It keeps dirt and germs out.

If you get a cut, skin can repair itself. That is because skin is always growing new **cells**. The older skin cells fall off. You lose thousands each minute.

♥ Your skin is the organ that protects your body.

WEIRD FACT!

Dust Mites! These tiny bugs live in dust. They are picky eaters. What do they eat? Your dead skin! As your skin flakes off, dust mites are ready to feast. They leave waste droppings behind as they eat. The droppings are dust mite poop. It gets into the air and can make people with allergies sick. *Achoo!*

Dust Mites

You are never alone. Tiny germs and **bacteria** are living on your skin. Eek! They can only be seen with a **microscope**. No need to worry. Most of them get along with you quite well. Not all of those little creatures are good though. Some can make you sick. How can you defeat the icky germs? Fight them off by washing and brushing your teeth. Soap, water, and toothpaste to the rescue!

♥ Those green blobs are bacteria that live on skin. You can't see them. A microscope was used to take this photo.

Your skin has millions of sweat glands. When your body gets too hot, those glands release sweat. The liquid is mostly made up of water. It leaves your body through tiny **pores** in your skin. Sweat turns into **water vapor** when it hits the air. Then poof—the heat is removed and your body cools down!

♥ Sweating helps people cool down on a hot day.

At first, sweat does not have an odor. It becomes smelly from bacteria. The tiny creatures feed on your sweat. They eat it! Then they leave acids behind. That is when sweat gets stinky.

WEIRD FACT!

Body Odor. The foods you eat can affect your odor. If you eat a large amount of garlic, be prepared. Your sweat may smell of garlic for days.

Skin does not work alone. It has help from your hair and nails. They protect your body too. Hair keeps your body warm. Eyebrows keep sweat from dripping into your eyes. Eyelashes and the hair inside your nose and ears keep dust out. Nails protect the tips of your fingers and toes.

Thin Skin!
Where is your skin the thinnest? On your eyelids!

Hair and nails are actually part of your skin. They are made of dead skin cells. (Yes, dead skin cells!) That's why it does not hurt when you trim them. If your hair and nails are dead, how do they grow? The part under the skin is alive.

♥ This drawing shows what lies below the epidermis which is the top layer of skin that you can see.

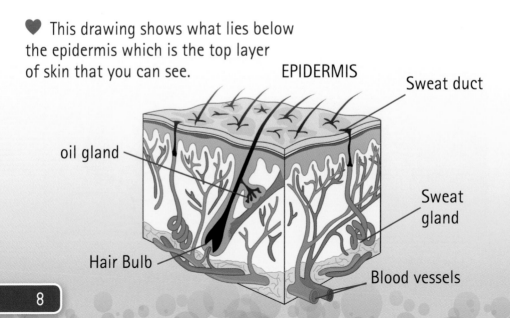

EPIDERMIS
Sweat duct
oil gland
Sweat gland
Hair Bulb
Blood vessels

Your skin is also home to oil glands. They release oil through your pores. The oil keeps your skin and hair from getting too dry. But wait, there's more! The oil also keeps water out and helps clear away dead skin cells.

Where do you have the most oil glands? Your face and scalp! When you become a teenager, your oil glands get busy. If a pore gets clogged with oil or dirt, a **pimple** may appear.

♥ Many teens get pimples. It's all part of growing up!

CHAPTER 2

Hands and Nails

Do you see why good hygiene is so important? Skin is covered with oil, sweat, dead skin cells, and bacteria. Add some dirt and germs. Now you have a real mess on your hands. In fact, germs on your hands can make you sick. If you put your hands in your mouth, the germs get a free ride to the inside of your body. That's where they can cause real trouble.

Instead, give those germs a proper goodbye. How? Wash your hands with soap and water to send them down the drain. Always wash after you use the bathroom. Wash before you prepare or eat food too.

TRY THIS!

Wash away germs!

Ask an adult to put a little baby oil or cooking oil on your hands. Rub it all over both sides of your hands. Have that person sprinkle a bit of baby powder (or flour) on your hands too. Pretend that the powder spots are germs. Follow the steps on the next page to wash them off.

Suds up the right way! Washing your hands works best if you do a good job. Follow these steps when you wash.

1. Turn on the faucet. Make sure the water is warm.

2. Get your hands wet.

3. Put soap in your hand.

4. Rub your hands together for 15 to 20 seconds. Sing the "Alphabet Song" to time yourself. *A, B, C, D...* Wash the front and back of each hand. Remember to wash your wrists, between fingers, and under your fingernails.

5. Rinse your hands under the water.

6. Dry your hands with a clean towel.

7. If you use a public bathroom, turn off the water with a paper towel. Open the door using the same towel. Then throw it away after you leave.

Where is a tricky place for dirt and germs to hide? Under your fingernails! (Germs are very sneaky.) Wash with soap and water. You can also use a nail brush with soft-bristles to clean under your nails.

Trim your nails often. Short nails are easier to keep clean. Use nail scissors or clippers to cut nails straight across. File the corners so they are rounded. Ask an adult if you need help.

♥ Keeping your nails trimmed and short will help keep them clean.

DID YOU KNOW?

Never bite your nails or pick at the skin around your nails. If your skin has a cut, germs can find their way inside. Your skin may get an infection. Infections are bad. Healthy skin is good. You get the idea.

Clap your hands! You have just taken care of your fingernails. Now look down at your feet and wiggle those toes. They are asking for attention. ("Down here! Look at us. Look at us!") Don't ignore them. They need to be cleaned and trimmed too.

Use nail clippers to trim your toenails. Cut straight across to make your toes happy. If not, you could get an **ingrown toenail**. That is when the nail grows into the skin. It hurts and can get infected. Use a file if you need to round the edges.

FUN FACT!

Nails! Fingernails grow faster than toenails. And your fingernails grow even faster if you are a kid.

CHAPTER 3

Body Basics

What do you get when you mix sweat, oil, and bacteria? Body odor or B.O. for short. The armpits are often to blame. Private parts (the **genitals** and **anus**) give off body odor too. Not to worry. Body odor is easy to remove by washing.

It's your choice—you can take a bath or a shower. Just make sure to wash regularly. Older kids should bathe or shower every day. Younger kids may not have to wash as often.

♥ As you get older, it's important to bathe every day.

Wash everywhere—from your head to your toes. Use your favorite soap or body wash. Put the soap on a washcloth or bath sponge. Then suds away! Make sure you wash your armpits and private parts. You may want to avoid using scented soap. The scents can irritate sensitive skin.

♥ Be sure to wash all parts of your body.

TAKE A TIP

Hot water can make your skin dry. Try using cooler water. If your skin is dry, you can put on lotion before you get dressed.

Have you ever smelled the inside of your shoes? Warning— it may be stinky! You may notice that your socks are wet after you wear them. The wet stuff is sweat. Bacteria are happy to dine on foot sweat. That can lead to some funky-smelling feet.

When you are washing your body, don't forget your feet. Wash the tops and bottoms of each foot. Also wash between your toes.

♥ Ewwww. Stinky sneakers come from sweaty feet.

Now hear this! That yellow stuff inside your ears is wax. It helps keep dust out of each **ear canal**. Glands in the ear canal are always making wax. Older wax usually falls out of the ears when it dries up. If the wax builds up, it may bother you. In that case, ask a doctor how to remove it safely.

Washing your ears is a snap. When you are in the shower, just wash the outside with soap and water. Dry off the ears with a towel. You can also use a cotton swab to dry the outside of your ears.

♥ You can use a cotton swab to dry the outside of your ears. But never stick a cotton swab into an ear canal. You can damage the **eardrum**. You may also end up pushing the wax deeper into the ear canal.

Hair can get quite dirty. Your scalp sweats and releases oil. Too much oil can make your hair greasy. Dead skin cells build up on the scalp too. That is why it's important to wash your hair. Rub your hair with water and shampoo. Then rinse.

How often should you wash your hair? It depends on your hair type. Hair that is straight and oily may need to be washed daily. Dry or curly hair may only need to be washed once or twice a week.

♥ People with oily hair need to shampoo more often than people with dry hair.

DID YOU KNOW?

Head Lice! These tiny bugs live on people and make their home on the scalp. They bite and can make your head very itchy. Lice spread easily from person to person. That is why you should never share a brush, comb, or hat. You don't want to give lice a free ride to your scalp.

Are you done with your bath or shower? (You've been in there for a long time.) Rinse well to remove any soap and shampoo. Then dry off with a towel.

You are growing up. Armpits begin to smell more as you get older. That is why people often apply **deodorant** after washing. It kills bacteria and will keep your armpits smelling fresh. (Did you notice the word *odor* in *deodorant*?)

♥ As kids get older, their armpits begin to smell. Some young people use deodorant to get rid of the stink.

Wait a minute! Are you putting dirty clothes on your clean skin? Eek! Dirty clothes can be covered with sweat and bacteria. Start each day with clean underwear and socks. Then choose the rest of your clean clothes. That will help you look, smell, and feel your best.

♥ Washing clothes regularly gets rid of sweat and bacteria.

Sleeping on clean sheets is a part of good hygiene too. Experts say it's best to change them every week. Don't wait more than two weeks though. Bedding gets dirty and sweaty too. That can cause bacteria to grow. Dead skin cells also end up in your bed. They make a tasty snack for dust mites.

DID YOU KNOW?

Dust Mites! Dust mites can be found living in your mattress. In fact, the average used mattress is home to millions of the tiny creatures.

Your face is unique. Show off that fabulous face by keeping it clean. Wash before bed with soap and water. Then pat dry with a clean towel. It's so easy you could do it with your eyes closed.

Speaking of eyes… In the morning, you may notice a bit of gunk in the corners of your eyes. The gunk can be sticky or crusty. It is made up of oil, dead skin cells, and **mucus**. (Gross!) During the day, your eyes blink and wash the gunk away. At night, it collects. Just wash with water to clean your eyes. You can also use a warm washcloth.

♥ Wash your face morning and night.

CHAPTER 4

Let's Talk Teeth!

Smile! Check out your teeth. They do a lot of work. Your chompers help you chew food. *Crunch. Crunch.* They also help you speak and sing clearly. *Fa, la, la!* Say *cheese*. Notice that you need your teeth to say the *ch* and *s* sounds.

Open your mouth. You can see your teeth, gums, and tongue. What don't you see? Millions of bacteria! They don't just live on your skin. Bacteria live inside your mouth too. They like warm, moist places. Some bacteria can damage teeth and gums. They can cause gum disease and cavities. A cavity is a hole in a tooth. Bacteria can also make your breath smell bad.

DID YOU KNOW?

Counting Teeth. By age 3, most kids have 20 teeth. They are called baby teeth. They start to fall out around age 6. Why? Adult teeth push the baby teeth out of the way. Most adults have 32 teeth. Count your teeth. How many do you have?

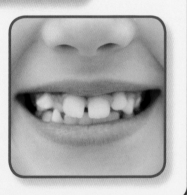

How can you keep your teeth clean? Brush them at least twice a day—in the morning and before bedtime. Use a small toothbrush with soft bristles. Put a pea-sized drop of toothpaste on the brush. Then gently brush your teeth. Clean the insides, outsides, and flat surfaces. Brush your tongue too. Bacteria also hang out there.

♥ Put a timer in the bathroom. Use it to make sure you are brushing for two to three minutes.

Don't rush when you brush! Take your time. Doing a good job takes two to three minutes. Replace your toothbrush every three to four months. The bristles get worn out.

Brushing alone is not enough. Bacteria are sneaky. They can hide in places where your toothbrush may miss. Use **floss** to clean between your teeth and along your gum line. Floss gently once a day to keep the bacteria away.

♥ Ask a grown-up to show you how to floss your teeth.

Visit the dentist every six months. A **dental hygienist** will clean your teeth. He or she may also take special photos called **X-rays**. They show the inside of your teeth. The dentist will study the pictures to make sure your teeth are healthy.

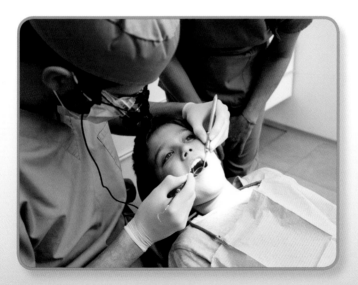

♥ Dentists can help keep your teeth and gums in good shape. A good rule is to see your dentist twice each year.

What else can you do to keep your pearly whites healthy? Eat foods that are good for you. Milk, cheese, and yogurt contain calcium. Calcium makes your teeth stronger. Munch on apples and raw carrots too. Eating raw fruits and vegetables cleans your teeth.

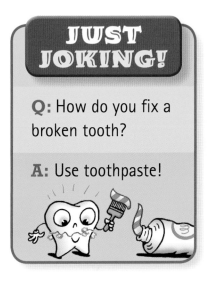

Try to eat fewer sweets. Foods like candy, dessert, and soda contain sugar. They may be tasty, but can damage teeth. Those troublemaking bacteria love sugar. They gobble it off your teeth. Then they leave acid behind. It's the acid that eats away at your teeth.

Wow! You look and smell fantastic. It must be all of that good hygiene. Keep it up! A clean body is a healthy one. It will also make you feel great. That should put a smile on your clean face. Well look at that—even your teeth are sparkling!

♥ Smile! It's easy to take good care of yourself.

What You Can Do!

How many of these rules do you follow?
Count the number of things you do.
See how you score below.

You . . .

1. wash your hands before eating.
2. scrub and trim your fingernails.
3. wear clean underwear each day.
4. take baths or showers regularly.
5. use shampoo to clean your hair.
6. wash your hands after using the toilet.
7. brush your teeth at least twice a day.
8. floss your teeth once each day.
9. wash your face before bedtime.
10. visit the dentist every six months.

If you answered "yes" to . . .

* **eight or more**—Great job keeping clean!

* **five to seven**—You are almost there.

* **one to four**—Keep trying. You can do it!

Glossary

anus: the open area in a person's bottom

bacteria: a kind of germ

cells: tiny building blocks of each living thing

dental hygienist: a worker trained to clean people's teeth

deodorant: a product that prevents body odor

ear canal: the passage inside each ear that leads to the eardrum

eardrum: a thin piece of skin inside the ear that vibrates when sound hits it

floss: thread that cleans between teeth and along the gum line

genitals: the male penis and female vagina

hygiene: keeping clean to stay healthy

ingrown toenail: a toenail that grows into the skin

microscope: an instrument that allows people to see a larger image of a tiny object

mucus: a slimy liquid produced by parts of the body

organ: a body part that has a certain function

pimple: a small swollen spot on the skin

pores: tiny holes in the skin

water vapor: water in the form of a gas

X-rays: special photos that show the inside of the body

What Did You Learn?

See how much you learned about keeping clean.
Answer *true* or *false* for each statement below.
Write your answers on a separate piece of paper.

1 The biggest organ of the body is the skin.
True or false?

2 Bacteria like to live in cool, dry places.
True or false?

3 Hair and nails are made of dead skin cells.
True or false?

4 Oil glands keep your skin from getting dry.
True or false?

5 Some kinds of sugar can protect your teeth.
True or false?

Answers: 1. True, 2. False (Bacteria like to live in warm, moist places.) 3. True, 4. True, 5. False (All sugar can damage your teeth.)

For More Information

Books

Baines, Rebecca. *Your Skin Holds You In*. The National Geographic Society, 2008.

Green, Jen. *Skin, Hair, and Hygiene* (Your Body and Health). Aladdin Books Ltd, 2006.

Manning, Mick. *Wash, scrub, brush!* Albert Whitman & Company, 2001.

Miller, Edward. The Tooth Book: *A Guide to Healthy Teeth and Gums*. Holiday House, 2008.

Shaefer, Valorie Lee. *The Care and Keeping of You: The Body Book for Younger Girls*. American Girl, 2012.

JUST JOKING!

Q: Did you hear the shoe joke?

A: You don't want to—it stinks!

Web Sites

American Academy of Dermatology
http://www.aad.org/dermatology-a-to-z/for-kids

Mouth Healthy Kids
http://www.mouthhealthykids.org

Healthy Teeth
http://www.healthyteeth.org/

KidsHealth: Skin (movie)
http://kidshealth.org/kid/htbw/skin-movie.html

BAM! Body and Mind
http://www.cdc.gov/bam/body/buzz-scuzz.html

Note to educators and parents: Our editors have carefully reviewed these web sites to ensure they are suitable for children. Web sites change frequently, however, and we cannot guarantee that a site's future contents will continue to meet our high standards of quality and educational value. You may wish to preview these sites and closely supervise children whenever they access the Internet.

Index

About the Author

Rachelle Kreisman has been a children's writer and editor for many years. She wrote hundreds of classroom magazines for *Weekly Reader*. Those issues included health topics about nutrition, illness prevention, sports safety, and fitness. When Rachelle is not writing, she enjoys being active. She likes taking walks, hiking, biking, kayaking, and doing yoga.